Beech Blurt

Poems by

Robert Edwards

Burble

By the same author:

Attitude to Sussex

Brighton Burble

Bridge Bluster

Photographs and cover design by the author

ISBN 0 9525909 6 4
Copyright © Robert Edwards 2004

Published by Burble, 12 Marine Square,
Brighton, BN2 IDL

Printed by Carmichael & Co Ltd,
Brighton, Sussex, England

Printed on recycled material

*British Library Cataloguing in Publication Data. A catalogue
record for this book is available from the British Library.*

PREFACE

Until I was eighteen, I lived in a building surrounded by woodland, in a Sussex area of sands, clays and ironstone, variegated soils and complex land use. Among the self-seeding plant life, the broad-leaved trees dominated my childhood - particularly, and supremely, the beeches. Some stood over our garden. One was especially memorable, for its grandeur, the opportunities for play, and the affection and awe that I felt for it. It and most of the nearest, considered hazardous, were removed when I was about nine. Something of a new generation has now appeared there.

At the age of seventeen I wrote a poem about the trees. More recently I gradually built up the collection that forms this book. With one or two exceptions, the subjects are not champions, rarities or exotic variants, though I should like to have seen more. I am sorry there is so little about woodmanship and carpentry; and I remain perilously untutored in the botany.

I have vivid recollections of marvels in passing which never found their way into the poetry: the summer arcade between Camelford and Wadebridge; the tree fronting a Charmouth hotel; a colossus at Woburn (Daniel Defoe refers to the "great beech woods which surround the parks and cover the hills" at "Wooburn"); a group in the centre of Hertford; layers of brilliant orange at the foot of a big riverside tree at Christchurch Meadow; sooty trees in Barnsley and a wealth of beauty just outside the town; a great curving wall of foliage at the perimeter of Rambouillet; and the deciduous muddle studied from the train between Trieste and Ljubljana.

I am grateful to the following people: for accommodating me, Anne Clarke, Kath Rangeley, Brian Wood, Gill Black, Bill and Vicky Glen, Alan and Fiona Prosser and Bob White; for accompanying me, Gary Aiston, Chris Sansom, Andrew Hemming and Judith White; for their help and interest, Rupert Radcliffe-Genge, Sarah Gibbings, Jack Collins, Paul and Jacqui Gould, Matt and Shirley Bukowski; for her great help, Eileen Climpson; and for their enduring kindness, Gill Fleming and Shirley Collins. Once again, many thanks to everyone at Carmichael's.

R.E.

CONTENTS

Snow in Ladbroke Grove, London   9

Oakington, Cambridgeshire   10

Graves Park, Sheffield, Yorkshire   11

Redhill Graft, Surrey   11

House in Haarlem, Holland   12

Green Park, London   13

Highgate Hill, London   14

Hot Air at Ledbury, Herefordshire   14

Copper Beech at Leeds Castle, Kent   15

The Whitehills Public House, Northampton   16

Lesbury, Northumberland   16

Decoration, East Street, Chichester, Sussex   17

Greenwich Park, London   18

Congleton, Cheshire   18

Churchyard, Saffron Walden, Essex   19

Pollards in the Great Wood at Felbrigg, Norfolk   20

Aldbury, Hertfordshire   21

Southborough Common, Kent   21

Garden Hedge, Appleby-in-Westmorland, Cumbria   22

Quartet at Winchelsea, Sussex   23

Patcham Place, Brighton, Sussex   24

Beech Village, Hampshire   26

Beech Hill Village, Berkshire   26

Toys Hill, Kent   27

Council House Hedge, Addingham, Yorkshire   28

Snapshot of Pershore, Worcestershire   29

Sunny at Newmarket, Suffolk   29

Sidmouth, Devon   30

Hotel near Bath, Somerset   31

Oxford College and Council Houses   32

Meikleour Hedge, Perthshire, Scotland   33

Palace and Lake, Drottningholm, Sweden   35

Morrab Subtropical Gardens, Penzance, Cornwall   37

Summer Shower at Sezincote, Gloucestershire   37

Excursion to Helsingør, Denmark   39

Arcade at Crampmoor, Hampshire   39

Runnymede, Surrey   40

Turin, Italy   41

Frankley Beeches, Birmingham   42

Street Trees, Bonn, Germany   43

Dublin Gardens, Ireland   44

Rain in Ebbw Vale, Caerphilly, Wales   45

Bank, Hollingdean, Brighton, Sussex   46

Cowdray, Sussex   47

Houghton Hill, near Arundel, Sussex   48

Craven Arms, Shropshire   49

Llangollen, Denbighshire, Wales   50

Darlington, County Durham   51

Blackbrook, Staffordshire   52

Fountains Abbey, near Ripon, Yorkshire   52

Path on Reigate Hill, Surrey   53

Windbreak in Winter Sunset, Stamford, Lincolnshire   54

Savernake Forest, Wiltshire   55

Epping Forest, Essex   56

Forest of Dean, Gloucestershire   57

Chilterns, (Berkshire) Buckinghamshire (Hertfordshire)   58

Lyons-la-Forêt, (Seine-Maritime) Eure (Oise), France   60

Tram and Train in the Forêt de Soignes, Brussels, Belgium   62

Prague, Czech Republic   64

Search in Spain   67

Bedfordshire   68

Derbyshire   69

Sherwood Forest, Nottinghamshire   70

Lancaster   70

Dorset   71

Burnham Beeches, Buckinghamshire   72

Basel to Bern, Switzerland   73

Windsor Forest, Berkshire   74

Wiltshire   75

Warwickshire   76

Hampshire Downs   76

Charnwood Forest, Leicestershire   78

Girl Beech   78

ILLUSTRATIONS

Frankley Beeches   *4*

Saffron Walden   *19*

Felbrigg   *20*

Winchelsea   *23*

Runnymede   *40*

Cowdray   *48*

Savernake Forest   *55*

Prague   *65*

Hawkley Hanger   *77*

Forêt de Lyons   *80*

Snow in Ladbroke Grove

January 2003

Snow, whose partial thaw was quick,
Stays, in places one inch thick,
Packed in patches everywhere
By the fast re-freezing air.
Elevations' pastel blush
Glamorizes gutter slush
Grey along ice-crusted kerbs.
Air no breeze at all disturbs
Tingles to the skin. A dry
Light derives from soft chill sky.
Shoots shot from the outspread tree -
Delicate embroidery -
Set themselves into the light,
Silhouetted, strangely bright.
Pointing up, their curves' effect
Is untangled - only flecked.
Husks in dozen clusters hang
Darkest, in the road's raw tang.
Farther in, the branches twine,
Coiling clear and firm in line,
Weaving out a well-shaped crown,
Rounded out and arching down -
Risen at the ridge's top,
Standing on the deeper drop.
Half way up, the bole divides.
Over most north-facing sides,
Bark is marked by lines of snow,
Slow to melt or to let go -

Single strips of white on grey
Like enamel flat inlay.
Ivy coats the lower trunk,
Garden-rooted. Roots are sunk
Hidden by a balustrade
Captured in the beech's shade.

Oakington

January 2004

Standing in line,
The young little oak trees face
A full-grown beech.
They already form a lot of limbs.
The beech, replete
With midriff divisions, mimes
Maturity.

Close to a house,
Probably much older than
The house, and
At a very ordinary side,
A tree trunk sits
Rectangularly blocked and squashed,
Somehow achieved.

Graves Park, Sheffield

February 1988

The north east wind is cold and hard.
Below a sky of blue, white, grey,
A magpie walks. Last year's leaves lie
In the moss and in the rough
Dead tufts of grass. Above the open
Slopes and the curved cavernous
Woods, comes this peculiar tree.
Shaped by the divided trunk
Like a lily, or woman's legs
Or Henry Moore, it is creaking
Quite loud - as what would not be -
Cold, alone in February.

Redhill Graft

February 2001

The bark on the base
Is more broken, furrowed.
The join has a kind of tidiness
Calming the shock of transplant.

Slime, dry lime green, climbs,
Covering the trunk's north side.
A curvature, protuberance, backs
Under a contortion of major branching.

The crown is a canopy
Of gossamer mohair hangings, shocks
Held at length from the block of flats
And over the pavement and almost the road.

House in Haarlem
March 1988

Standing square in front of
A detached town mansion, the tree
Is mature, broad and sturdy.
Alone it fronts the pale facade.
The house is primrose yellow, and
The forecourt is a half moon lawn
Completely dominated
By this grand grandfatherly tree.
Two green lanterns at the door
Hang like gold-framed emeralds:
Eye-like lights behind the guard.
The tree is like an only child,
Now too old for that much
To signify. Something says
America.

Green Park

March 2001

Round past the Ritz
Resides one. It's
Shy, surprising,
Tantalising,
Very upright,
Hemmed in too tight.
Jostled, sheer class -
A champagne glass
In shape. In tone,
Strangely alone,
Embraced in this
Metropolis
By quite some huddle,
Bound to befuddle.
Below the waist
Is lost, untraced
Amid the growth,
Northern, hot, both,
Of other stuff -
The smart and rough,
Beyond the park.
The brown buds, dark,
Long, thin and high,
Point to the sky.

Highgate Hill
March 2001

Up over Highgate, compared with elsewhere
In London, the beeches are oddly not rare -
A pause in the scramble of random domain,
Sedately encased in a gravelly strain
Of clay, inconspicuous nevertheless
If not cultivated in Kenwood finesse.
Here to the east near the cemetary,
Shadowy looms a fantastical tree -
Symmetrical, muscular, solid, compact,
Full of a vertical forking all stacked
Into a tall candelabrum affair,
Painted in algae green - dark, gothic, bare.

Hot Air at Ledbury
May 2003

Sagging on a hillside,
Ledbury is lodged.
Through the straggled pathways
Beech above are wodged.
Right up on the ridge top,
Beefy silver grey,
One bulk seems to cool this
Dehydrating day.

Copper Beech at Leeds Castle, Kent

June 1993

A straight up side of trunk supports
The diametric opposite curvature
Combining up to verticality.

The broad low hub of living wood when
Seen from far is all the indication
Of the source and centre of the rest.

The majesty of mass, above, amazes.
Presumably these leaves, purple maroon,
Must be in the region of a million.

In the curling breezes latticed
Collations play perpetual realignments
In a wide sky of strong blue.

Curve, swerve, hoop and helm -
It is a model of ever so many's
Refinement - mould casting recreation.

The Whitehills, Northampton

June 2001

The trunk is a triangle, tapered -
Earth steeple - pasted, papered
Grey. Strife has brought a smudge -
Torn bark too deep to budge.
A children's playscape tree
Of comic majesty,
It serves down drunkenly
Its wounds and wizardry.

Lesbury

July 2003

The railway line,
Beyond the brine
At Alnmouth and
The salted land,
By fields brings near
A beech. We veer
Away, whereas
The place it has,
A standards' dearth,
Awards their worth.

East Street, Chichester

November 1999

High, heavy,
Pale grey,
A Georgian home
Steps back
From the street.
In front, feet
From the street,
The tree
Rises, held
Inward, hands
In pockets.
Hairy
Thin lines
Of long
Twig hang.
Sunlit golden
Leaves trickle
Intricate,
A shawl
Of lametta,
Chains
Of light
Fine lustre.

Greenwich Park

December 1987

Beneath it, we admire this tree
That perches threatening to ski.
Royal since 1433,
The belvedere bewilders me.
The beech tilts forward awkwardly -
A physique free from fantasy.

Congleton

December 2003

A mill-stream river meets a bridge of stone
Whose iron railings lend a civil tone
In black and white. Immediately close,
A big old beech is ample - almost gross.
The bank it stands on, like a landing stage
Or podium, flat-floored, highlights its age.
The crown's outline is like a spinning top:
In dizzy swirls massed shoots fly to a stop.
In essence its position is a squat;
Its patterning a massive crazy knot.
Low, loose, below the gnarled green-powdered tangle,
Is tied a tape - unprepossessing bangle.

Saffron Walden

December 2002

Beside a limbless chestnut tree,
Before a broad and tall church front
The beech is hospitality -
In small quaint streets its big bole blunt.

Solidly built and with a kink
Of self-adjustment: shifted shoulder;
Pale as the grey of a sheeted zinc
Article; fervent as art or holder.

Branches at ninety degrees all stoop
Streaming a quarter disc with floss
In clear definition of shoots; a group
Of rounded roots in rich green moss.

Pollards in the Great Wood at Felbrigg
January 2004

The lane turns sharply to the left and falls,
A kind of carving through the deep-set banks.
In parts the banksides face as sheer as walls,
And dip back down and up again - leaf tanks.
Along the bank tops, both sides of the lane,
Irregularly spaced, and mounted firm,
The aged trees if strange seem strangely sane.
They have outlasted beech's common term,
Their being mighty multi-poled. The bulk
Is conjured in a balance at the point
Of pollarding: sufflation from a hulk;
Enormities of burden in a joint.
And potency continues in their build.
With leaves, rich proof of productivity,
The ditches' troughs are flatly, densely filled.
The triple-trunks of every trophy tree
And quadruples and quintuples are long.
Odd orange lichen colours one. They are
All formidably tall, surviving, strong.
Whose log lies, cased in carpet moss, bizarre?

Aldbury

January 2002

Mid-January. Cold mid-afternoon.
Grey woolly clouds unravel. Drizzle falls.
Gradually the woods, colour of prune
Distinct against the sky, break into halls,
Approached below. Surprising - not to cloy,
But curiously lax: trees' agile forms
Feel free, unforced. They have a gentle joy,
Good-natured. Wintered observation warms,
Along the matt green moss, into the grass.
Below the lead-grey lid of cloud, a pale
Panel of turquoise blue appears, to pass
Exquisite light to decorate and scale
The trees. Bare branches let the light in. Deep,
Like rugs compiled of rich brown flakes, the leaves
Lie motionless in each round bowl and heap.
A raw north wind is sharp. Stillness deceives.

Southborough Common

March 2002

Undergrowth of holly
Flickers in the sun -
Like a mass of lolly,
Prone to overrun.
Ivy - darker, stiffer -
Crawls around and wraps
Tree trunks. Free trunks differ,
Starving long-laid gaps.
Winding paths, appearing
Arbitrary, lead
To a kind of clearing
Wealden beeches breed.

Garden Hedge, Appleby-in-Westmorland

March 1997

Alongside a steep straight path,
It is between -
Between itself and ideas of it;
Between a liquid Eden and Eden's
Very line of rail; and winter and spring:
Past and future - bronze whispers
In a light wind - last year's leaf life
Curled and done for and even now in March
Unshed. Tall and thin
It stands as a slice
Of crispness. One curving fan tail
Forms an arch, seamless, with an evergreen.

Quartet at Winchelsea

March 2002

Continental plans brought less to be
Widespread than the grass at Winchelsea.

Houses rise white-rendered on a grid
Two thirds of whose plots received no bid.

Pasture on the plateau deep impinges,
Magnetising sheep - the grazing binges.

Sharp up from the grass, oaks most, a gang
Serves the sweetest songbirds ever sang.

Centre stage, four beeches, greenish grey,
Fan out from the super-alluvial clay.

Two, one east one west, splay. Bent apart,
Both dimensions play in skylined art.

Through the hundred and eighty degree
Stick sketch flare, lies ridgelike, blue, the sea.

Patcham Place

April 2001

Chestnuts near by -
a few, between -
surprise the eye -
precocious green

whereas our friend,
already rigged -
rooks can suspend
a nest of twigged

and coarse haired wicker
at giddiest height -
is clothed no thicker
than when snow white.

Last year's, grey-brown,
some husks, unclenched,
befleck the crown,
defunct, unwrenched.

They are sixteen,
old beeches here -
and some have seen
a long career.

Black mansion's grove
of dignity
extends a town's
welcome with tree.

The first is one
grand siècle hunk
bodied by Poussin:
big-rippled trunk.

One stands away
some yards - alone -
an outfield stray,
the sunk field's own.

At mansion's front
are two mad trees.
One tilts - a stunt -
fifty degrees.

Beech Village, Hampshire
April 2003

We can well imagine here
Past hangers profuse.
The eponym now leans to
The commonplace, obtuse.
By nature and by number
The beeches hang thin
While, south several miles
Landed antiques glide in.

Beech Hill, Berkshire
April 2003

A few to be found in a wood at the east
And two that surround the church path, are pieced
Into the travelogue diligently.
Wild flowers - primrose, wood anemone,
Violet and lesser celandine -
Nestle near husks. They quietly shine.
Facing the wood is a five trunked beech
Assaulted by ivy and a jay's bright screech.
As to the name, forget *fagus*, think afresh:
To medieval French and a shield *de la Bêche*.

Toys Hill

April 2002

Land once left by Robert Toys
More than seven hundred years
Past, perches above the vale.
Sweet spring smells released by rain
Range on cold breeze. Ground enjoys -
Bared from scraping, flint appears -
Golden sandy pink. The pale
Beeches lurk near every lane,
Wooding heath in leanest noise
Quieter than a human hears.
Casualties of the gale,
Few from eldest beech remain.
Salutary teetered poise
Opens when a clearing nears.
Pillar forms prefigure frail
Destiny. But shoots contain
Buds uncurling plant alloys -
Leaves beginning long careers,
Flowers female, flowers male,
Fluff and fleck discharged in chain.

Council House Hedge in Addingham

May 2000

Fine eye-lash outlines
Edge - etch - light bright green
Leaves - pellucid - prime.

Downy dark brown shoots
Express the froth's bond
With inner life.

Ethereal silk
Floats, animating
Twigs and tauter limbs.

Silence meets a breeze -
Caress. Greater gusts
Effect a whisper.

The coat caves. Bony
Anatomy bends
Traced into the earth.

Snapshot of Pershore

May 2003

Peaceful, slow, the river bends,
Thickset in textured sides,
Westward. The road across it swerves
East. Peace with pace collides.
Climbing, the road relinquishes
The open fields below -
Entering the broken light
Thick summer beeches throw.

Sunny at Newmarket

May 2000

Whatever the foundings,
Whatever the aims,
They stuff the surroundings
With deep green flames.

Sidmouth

July 2000

Out, up from the small
And semi-regal sea-front,
Westish, west in effect -
We meet this. Precariously
Positioned, on a precipitous
Point, over the under-slope,
A cavalier figure appears.
Brilliant in pre-seasonal green
Costume, proclaiming, dizzy,
Flourishing lanky gestures
Down into the sweepy bay,
Backed by the shades,
Met for a moment,
Making an impression.
Gone further up, steep
Into some silver slender
Pipe entwining tunnel -
Dappling chequered sunlight
In green darkness,
An arch tunnel arbour -
We swivel to see.
Hair raisingly high,
Glimpsed in feathery gaps
Down there
Delerious into the sea
Sidmouth
Disappears
From out on the open dry grass,
Awkward brown cliffs
And dark spiry promontories.

Hotel Near Bath

July 2000

A summer evening, staged in scenes of stone
Presided over by a host of trees,
Intensifies the harmony of tone.
The trees appear to coexist with ease.
That combat which secured their survivals
Is lost for us - their scholarship, we groom.
Meanwhile among the safe maturer rivals
The orange lights of town lamps pierce their gloom.

At a shattered gatehouse turned hotel
South of the town, assorted trees are tall.
Serving an urbane purpose very well,
They reach, they rise, they tower. But not all -
Since two of them have been decapitated.
Unbusted, they are not undone. One's top
In brown-leaf bric-a-brac is decorated.
The wall upholds the other's lofted lop.

Oxford College and Council Houses

July 2000

Outside the city, around some higher slopes,
Common beeches can be commonly encountered.
Most are suave and svelte, in a common
Behaviour of beech. Some spread their high
Canopies over the road by Boar's Hill,
From where today the city fades
In a film of humid haze - ungilded.

Inside the city, they become uncommon.
Golden stone glows in dim light. Flat,
Formal gardens have trees, *viz*
The huge maroon patrician backcloth
Tucked in bricked Keble's quadrangle recess.

Along a road of simple houses - boxes -
Barely designed - comes a quite other
Quad recess, houses on three sides. Centred
On the empty flat dry grass ground,
A smaller copper beech seems almost
Apologetic. Well-shaped, with a wrung
Trunk, rather thirsty, its bold form has
Perfection.

Meikleour Hedge, Perthshire

July 2003

A dry stone wall of one to three feet high,
Earthed, underlies the northern corner. Here,
The hedge top, out of sight, is lost in sky.
The leaves are mostly rather small; and near,
Their composition bushy. Little gaps
Or holes appear along the way. Real trees
Emerge - true trunks. Wood chipping overlaps
The path - twigs, husks and bud scales. Fantasies
Reciprocate when signatures come carved
In bark. Graffiti, keen to tell the time,
Disfigure blunt initials, digits - halved
In depth by time. In causing eyes to climb,
They pull at the pedestrian. Light shoes
Tread shoots of bright green grass, and, leavened, spring
In soft black loamy earth; and then they lose
Firm tread in drifted leaves. An opening
Much like a doorway suddenly appears.
An opportunity to step inside
Presents itself. Most curious of rears -
The colonnade of trees shadily spied.
Allowed to branch, their backs assimilate
To ordinary woodland habitat.
Re-entered, hedgeside viewpoints intimate
A certain loss of innocence. Less flat,
The overall impression is a row
Of bow fronts. Further south, its weave invokes
In altered light a rough and furry flow.

A light breeze ruffles, faster traffic strokes,
The surface of the lower part. Thick, dense,
The central range, less perforated, stands
Most like a wall or wooden wired fence,
The leafwork so compressed. Vertical bands
Are indistinguishable. Then some thin
Grey columns in this midst parade the spines.
Towards the southern end, some ail - their skin
Cracked, peeling. Many more are fit. Like vines,
Twig shoots entwined are twenty feet in length,
And broadly splayed, and scarcely more than one
Small centimetre's width. Hence is the strength
Transmitted from the trunks direct. They run
At frequent intervals. Obliquely set,
The final block's mild gradient falls short
Of two fine rivers beautifully met.
Through Perthshire, beech thrives, howsoever brought.

Palace and Lake, Drottningholm

July 1997

This tree is as firm and solid as a Swede
But somewhat knobbly -
Not a lot of sleekness
Except the silver instead of gold skin.

I feel some leaves in my left hand.

We picnic under a neighbouring tree.
Out from a cream stone palace outhouse
Come two handsome
Royal guards in royal blue uniform.

(Is Elizabeth Söderström here?)

Their manner is not at all military,
But their confidence is complete
As, almost as it were confiding, they
Direct us off their dusty summer grass.

Elsewhere grass is thick and tall.

A dense or distant wilder walk from here,
Over an island inlet bend of Mälaren,
A forest bank promontary falls
Into the lake - cornered quiet land.

Litterless - a seldom passing boat.

The lake to the east is large and spreads
Away. Turning west the broad channel
Feels less pressing to the shoreline land,
The inland archipelago.

From the grass and thickets, through the pines -

Talking and smiling, mildly matter of fact,
Treading the steep tiered smooth round brown
Rocks: relaxed, four naked gold tanned men,
Two at a time, flip to dive -

Dropping like dolphins into the deep clear water.

Just above the water, between sand
And pools, pines and bush, growing
From a crevice in the rocks, a beech
Confronts the brilliant sunlight.

The tree safeguards my body from the sun.

It is of hardly more than human scale,
A gathering of steady twigs,
Carrying full scatterings of leaves,
Tickling extended interruption.

Morrab Subtropical Gardens, Penzance

July 2000

In the moist and warm wood-chipped soil,
As locals these two are not all alone.
In a cosmopolitan community of species,
The odd oak and birch and so on inhabit
The perimeter. But these do play a most
Remote and secret role. In an open arena
Exhibiting exotica, high, low, palmy,
Balmy these beeches hide in a shaded
Corner, cosy, plebeian. Sweet warmth
Obtains between the two. They respond
Spaciously to an inquisitive upheld hand.

Summer Shower at Sezincote

August 1996

By a busy quiet cotswold lane stands,
Quietest of notices, with simple
Sky blue lettering, a small
White painted worn wooden waymark.

The house is a frame of golden flame
Shelved on the long east-facing hill,
Speaking, or sparkling, of spas.

She is a pleasing object of resort,
The classical creature
Whose eagle-backed body and voluptuous
Bust supports the fountain - though all
Her surface and her garment or garb
Are in a sorry old, sorry, old state.

Arrives a very heavy rainfall
As one reads by foot the paths
That comment down the pool side turf.

One shelters in a shade of weeping beech
So crooked some of its branches
Are propped with posts. Incredibly
Effective is this dome - green igloo
Arbour, keeping, containing one
Practically dry.

But we cannot wait. We plod-hop
Through the elderly women stuck
On the stepping stones
Under the bridge.

At the top of the oriental garden
A beech, above the palm and smoke bush,
Could not be shaped more different
From the hospitable weeper -
Three times as tall,
Almost like a conifer in form.

Excursion to Helsingør

August 1998

The plain train, a Dane train,
Chunky-bodied, hard silver-blonded
Skin, makes off with its
Mixture of commuter and punter custom.

It stops at every station.
The sea is never far, and
For quite a while, never seen.
Then it has that riviera habit.

Dark blue Baltic brightly calms one's eyes.
Only now, nearly at the hour's end,
Crowds of beeches rise around the line -
A green forest glinting against the sea.

Arcade at Crampmoor

August 2001

Name plates, like residential lane plates, long,
Placed low, in black on white, true, cool and strong,
Pronounce and point - Straight Mile. The trees behave
As though to copy a cathedral nave.
A day too hot and bright to dim the sky
Lets apertures dehumidify.
Leaves' tissue steels. They curl while shoots can ladle,
Accentuating how some branches cradle.
Along the sky the arching stoops to meet -
Vaultings whose vertices are incomplete.

Runnymede

September 2001

The river turns, rightangular.
The weight of water rears, not far
Away from which the languid flow
Is lost below the land from view.
The field is flat and most of its
Perimeter is asterisked
By plotted beeches. Their first role
Is balancing the towered bulk
Of trees that crowd the bank across.
Particularly pointed, one,
Close to the bank, with room for robes,
In light aplomb personifies
Mutation in complexion's look.
Maroon from half a mile away
While green becoming golden close,
It has a kind of arrogance
Of pedigrees preserved and crossed.

Turin

September 1999

Into the *Giardini Reali*
The orange trams trail
A serpentine curve
Along the path
Shaded by trees.
The few beeches
Are dark, dull.
One stands deep
In dust and husks,
With no roots wandering,
But branches
Hung enough
To be reached
On foot
By hand,
Feeling floppy,
Like thin leather,
And so dark.

In an innermost
City piazza,
Green gardened,
By deafening traffic
And bogged in smog -
Some beeches
Improbably cower:

Their leaves a little
Smaller, lighter, golder,
Their figure
More pointed,
Their fortune
More pinched.
The grimy
Colonnaded and balconied
Orange buildings crowd
Rigid,
Cloying.

Frankley Beeches

September 2003

A clump to be considered
Equally a club,
The trees, about two hundred,
Top an upturned tub.

They stand straight on a hillock,
Genteel, by the sprawl
Of Birmingham, and banish
Underscrubweed brawl.

So hot and long the summer,
Ground is deeply dry.
Alive, a leaf mosaic
Plates the shuttered sky.

Street Trees, Bonn

September 2003

For seventeenth to nineteenth
Centuries the suburb stands,
Peaceful, domestic, serious,
Close to the commercial centre,
Separated by the train station.

Birches cascade, cypresses rule
Over *Beethovenplatz.* Eccentric
And brash is the ash, cornered
Where lone-limed *Handelstrasse*
Meets *Haydnstrasse's* chestnuts.

By *Bachstrasse,* poplar towers
Queue at a moment's modernity.
In the street a silver maple's
Leaves hang lacy, pointed, limp.
Sycamore, copper beech coexist.

Town-housed, launched in roses,
The pavements of a narrow street
Contain forty greenleaf beeches,
Rugged long-stemmed trumpet-bowl
Goblet lines: on *Mozartstrasse.*

Dublin Gardens

October 2003

Rafter shafts of late afternoon
Sunlight, low from sky-line roofs,
Driven into tree tops, light
St Stephen's Green. Curves comprising
Brown, orange, yellow, green
Stand out, reflected in some dark
Water: the beech, a tall triangle,
Swoops toward's the ground and water.
Fifty metres across the green
On a short thick bank beside
The water, an old and immensely broad
Beech trunk breaks into six or seven
Branches wilfully individual.

In the misty morning drizzle,
Serene, the terraced brick's approach
To Fitzwilliam Square reveals
Beeches in the garden - vaulted,
Three on the west side, three on the east.
Brown-green layers are gently lifted
And lowered by brief slow breezes. Bright
Copper and fudge coloured shell-shape leaves
Gather on the street ground. Near,
Merrion Square's one signal beech,
In the south west corner, lets
Pale grey noon light through an even
Parasol of orange sprigs.

Rain in Ebbw Vale

October 1989

Dripping from deciduous canopies
And seeping through undergrowth,
Shining off a ragged road,
Rain, falling like strands of wool,
Drenches the hidden soil.

The drop to the dingle
Is deep and sharp.
The bank
To this other side
Is darker in the underview
Of the density of wood.

Out of the woods
On the mountain top
The church and chapel
And the farm and house
Are grey
Like the damp sky softened
With the whiteness of a tavern.

The lane claws
Narrow
Twists
Into the village
And the steep stony terraces.

The A road rests along the flat:
A ledge constructed along the hidden
River.

The road crawls like a sea diver
Towards the broad light, passing
Hundreds of beeches
Tumbling in tiers
Over the fast river,
Blazing with golden leaves,
Bowing with wilful insecurity
And ineradicable defiance.

Hollingbury Bank, Hollingdean
October 1988

For twelve months having lain
Along the bank, colossal sticks,
They do not roll down. Kept on land
In life their home, they keep in fact
Their colour, bark unbroken, leaden
In light dim, platinum under sun.
Some, either alive or dead,
Supine, appear to contemplate the sky -
Asleep - superb.

Cowdray

November 2001

Along the lowering lilting slopes
Affecting views over the vale,
A line of southward vision lopes
Leaping to meet a montane trail.

In groups and isolate they stand,
Some diminished by bane or streak,
On the grass, in dark red sand,
Leaf-mould and new-fallen litter - sleek.

Grey bristled husks and bright brown mast
Lie among the roots and moss.
The contents of the nuts has fast
Turned to black powder, lavish in loss.

By a pale grey stump has grown
Leathery fungus dark and broad.
We can but wish it well alone
And trust few sites could such afford.

Houghton Hill

November 2001

High above Arundel, grasses and scrub
Flourish. Old pathways run from a hub,
Houseless but homely. Surrounded by trees,
The clearing is dotted with woodposts - keys.
Openings obvious, others obscure,
Beckon. The bright lantern hangings' allure -
Oranges, yellows, greens and browns -
Devour the entrant. High on the downs,
The beeches envelop. All is in shade.
The feeling of reeling, the sense that one strayed,
Heightens. Mighty spectres loom.
Thickset specimens make more room.
One has a warmth and vitality. Then,
One, seeming senior in the den,
Rears like a bear, old and weary -
Decorated in something eerie,
Bee-shaped, woolly netting, black
Accretions - off the beaten track.

Craven Arms, Shropshire

November 2003

The rain prevents one seeing well
The scenery. Out of the flat
Erupt the rocks. One cannot tell
Much more than outlines, nervous at
The nature of an ordovician
Corridor. Strangely sublime,
The sharp smooth slopes impart fruition -
Late autumn, early winter time.
Berries and buds and pale grass plume
Overlay a husk on shades
Of salmon in some dusky bloom.
Along the flat, a land hand aids
The space of oak - and beech. The stalks
Rise from the fields abrupt like bone,
Long boles as plumb as bottle corks.
At Craven Arms one stands alone.
Unlikely form to thrill or freshen,
The branches lilt. Weary they fall,
Moody and moist in dimmed impression,
Dolorous and downward all.

Llangollen

November 2003

Rapidly the river flows,
Jumping into crests.
It rolls and stumbles on the stones
In mutual arrests.
Above its bend, the quarry gapes.
Above the quarry, grey,
The bare stone, sometimes vertical,
From white mist climbs away.
Serrated by its darkened firs
The rock top, higher still,
Is densely clouded. Here, a man
And dog descend the hill.
The beeches are a funny looking
Lot, bark roughened, weird.
Shoots and branches crane and lurch
Peculiarly steered.
Some contort divided trunks
Trapped in a self-made lock.
Some up higher seem to grow
Dry out of the rock.
Pale green fern and multi-toned
Moss grow on the floors.
Fallen leaves are luminous
Among the sycamores'.
Twenty metres from the river,
Soft straight symmetry
Fans out from a smooth beech trunk
Of stone grey gravity.

Darlington

December 2003

On empty, open meadow slopes
Fine lineaments flounce.
Associated gestures' hopes
Analogies renounce.

Down in the parish church-yard by
The river, nineteen graves'
Old headstones, shaded, half belie
How history behaves.

Up in the shopping centre, on
A corner at the edge,
A solid column's peace has gone,
But little of its pledge.

Blackbrook, Staffordshire

November 2003

A few miles from the village Beech,
And angularly broad,
A platform, raked, supports a wood,
Radiantly floored
In leaves of golden brown, sunlit,
Striking and inviting.
The open airy lie of land
Is green to foot the flighting.

Fountains Abbey

December 1988

Huge in the long and happy frame these
Crowding round in groups, lines and
Clusters, overlook the ambling humanity
Made miniature. Some seem tired. All
Work, in their own time, at leisure as
Instruments of timeless enlightenment.
Though much we may injure the world so
Insulting ourselves, we can do this well.
We thirst for landscape as handsome
As this, as between bitter by can or
Wine by decanter we capture springwater.

Path on Reigate Hill

December 2001

In the middle of a day
In late December, the south sky
Is almost summer blue. The blue
Pales into the southerly white.
Half way on the North Downs Way
The upward path saunters by
The scarp. Forming a quirky queue
To stare, wandering sheep invite
Visual advice. The grey
And charcoal ram turns back. Crows cry.
Beeches reign. A mighty few
Raise many arms. Massive, or slight,
Roots run riot through overlay
Of moss and husks. All of them lie,
Long arabesque or log askew,
In leaves - damp velvet layers. Quite
Soon the strength and piercing play
Of light subsides. To west, the eye
Sees against silver, sealed buds new.
A robin rests - then springs to flight.

Lincolnshire Windbreak in Winter Sunset

December 2002

Deep dark piles of mauve grey cloud
Skirt all horizon skies.
Fierce low sunlight bathes plain bark
In copper pink disguise.

Trees are straggled from north to south
Behind an old long wall.
Air is cold. The trees are old,
Beeches best glowing of all.

Savernake Forest

April 2003

Here there are many, protected and free,
Prodigiously quaint. Extraordinary.
Their roots are smooth, rounded and burrow below.
Bell-bottomed trunks up from dimpled shins grow.
Inwardly curved, a symmetrical waist
Supports lengthy arms whose gravity, based
Far from each forearm and farther from wrist,
Seems by mere balance their weight to subsist.

Epping Forest

May 2001

Soft brown banks in folds and rolls
Lob and lift divergent boles,
Quickly hilling. The slim low
Tract, languid as ridges go,
Grants an opportunity.
Beeches fancy, beeches free,
Root in acid topsoil. Oaks -
More low lying, more like blokes -
Long related, let them by.
Hornbeams, chief teams here, comply.
Months of tension culminate
When, this week, the shoots create
Out of buffed and brown-gold pins,
Leaves and flowers. Bursting skins
Climax into curling sheen -
Pale, almost insipid green.

Forest of Dean
May 2003

Cinderford - bare,
Stricken by industrial denial,
Skids on a tall
Tip, and shuns the no more mercantile
Severn, below,
Looping, somnolent. Further from there
And around, hills
Fill a fading territory where
Outlines are smooth,
Hiding sharp and complex shapes. Close, down
Into the woods,
Mindful of past mining out of town,
You find a fierce
Density of shade. The bluebells glimmer.
Ferns throng confused.
Gathered close together, trees are dimmer.
Is this a raven
Slackened in its langour on a gate?
One massive beech
Stands in open grass, a mighty weight,
Half down a hill,
Surrounded by mixed woodland forestry,
Crowded. A clean
Red-floored, cloistered, chambered company,
Pure beech allure,
Entices by enchantment to retreat.
Ruardean: a low
Row leans - gorged, the winding Wye to meet.

Chilterns

May 2001

A mile or two to Marlow Bridge
And close upon the Thames,
The land falls like some stairwell, and
The landings' trees are gems.

Above the harsh escarpments, there
Are windbreaks where among
Some conifers, deciduous
Companions are young.

The darkness in the densities
That drop from Cadmore End
Can be less inhospitable
Where shade space can befriend.

- Or go into the undergrowth -
Adventure if inclined.
Nature no less creates the beech,
Impulsive or resigned.

These look athletic, half of them,
As though out on a walk -
Through bluebell dark display of light -
In clay lain on white chalk.

A greenest piece of London's belt,
From Chorleywood, north-west
Along the ridge to Amersham,
Of both worlds has the best.

A beech stands by the main ridge way.
It faces, isolated,
Its kind across the deep fields,
Multitudinously mated.

All quality in quantity
Challenges common sense.
Beauty in bland abundance
Requires recompense.

Apart from faults intrinsic,
Curiosity suggests
Detail - the inexhaustibles.
Detail barely rests.

The worst of every winter seems
To take somehow too long,
Whereas the haste of early summer
Scheduling seems wrong.

The beech leaves lose their silk and sheen
And harden into colour
So rich, acidic, it would be
A crime to call it duller.

Forêt de Lyons

May 2002

East in higher Normandy,
Fields fall verdant, land clear-cut,
Propped or cropped, contrasted,
Neatly jointed, streamed in soft-side
Pastures, reeds. Cattle and horses
Cogitate. Verges, clipped
Beside thin lanes and smooth road
Stretches, flank unexpected
Bends. Foreseen somewhat, beeches
Tower together, flanging woods.
Open air perimeters
Produce abundant buttercups.
The woods outwit the eye, dumbfounding
Summation - late spring forestry
Fecund. Surprisingly fertile,
Soil of the surface grows thick grass,
Nettles, brambles, fern, sporadic
Moss: ankle roots are often
Muffled. Across the plateaux, levels,
Dips, hard husks are settled on
Leafmould melting into mash.
Beeches gather everywhere,
Some keeping quite peculiar
Politeness in their spacing. They
Rise like warping sticks of rock
Or rhubarb, silver, seldom tilting.
Many seem of a similar age,

And stylised, uniform,
Blooms like green geraniums
With flake-form branches
Flaring shoots profusely high.
Long and bare and everywhere
Trim sideless trunks explode
In foliage at shoulder point,
Outstretched and intertwining.
Younger ones provide tiers
More busy-branched or bushy-rimmed.
Sumptuous in bright sunlight,
Dappled lantern patchwork gleams
Occasionally broaden, bringing
Volumes of arrested light.
Beeches, thousands, tens of thousands,
Integrate like stems of grass.
Lost among their numbers' lines,
Amalgamating, specimens
Disperse. Dark topsoil drags the eye
Down. Tracks, dry and wide, detract,
Divide. In time, interior
Perspectives enter open sky.
Outlying, outstanding, old
Trees excel. Proximity
To forestry's exterior
Seems to save maturity.
Fat and looking fit, one
Stands like some retired guard,
A warmly formal welcomer.

Tram and Train in the Forêt de Soignes

May 2003

The tram track
Is a shallow sunken
Path of patted
Red brown earth,
Lightly gravelled.
Reaching a little
Away from the roads
The tram swings
Into a figure S,
Creaking, rocks
A brief way up
In beech wood banks,
A long line down,
Turning around
Among the trees
At Tervuren.
Young leaves lilt,
Sweet light green -
Treacle tawney
Hinted in
The endurance
Of unfurled scales.

The train pulls out
Of Boitsfort Bosvoorde
Going to Groenendaal.
Two beeches appear
High on a bank,

Low in prolonged
Pilaster grip.
Vertical branches
From rightangles run
Into apparent
Expansive crowns.
Inside their park
They are seen to be
Decapitated.

The train rushes past
Hollows and small
Hillsides and slanting
Plateaux - ash, birch
And oak outnumbered
By serried beech. Trees
Tear away from
Window-worn eyes
In a commotion,
Sliding aside,
Fleeting in file. Split
By realms of history,
And by reason
Of roles, they represent
Kingdoms and courts,
Provincial authorities,
Venture to vending -
Estate re-trained
In paths of patronage.

Prague

May 2001

Slavonics articulate without articles
Indefinite or definite. So -
In morning sun on *Letna* Park,
Strong south breeze lifts lined with river.
Compartments of tiny tourists inch
Across Charles Bridge. Steeples and domes
Are silhouetted in east. In west,
They bask in sun. Bell,
Melancholy muted harsh, bangs.
Funny beech, fifteen metres high,
Seems to have been hammer-tapped
Into ground - few roots visible.
Very thin silver branches all
Stick sideways in oblique
Zigzag forms from fair-sized bole
Smoothly dimpled. Scattering of tree's
Yellow grey flowers is numerous
On flat floor which it shades.

On dark bank of cutting
For trams and cars parting
Letna from Garden, soil appears
To be softer, trees taller. Close to clump
Of copper beeches, tucked among ash
And sycamore, one common beech
Stands on slope - tender, slender, firm,
Bare, branchless until crown, high and light.

Royal Palace Gardens proper produce
Two pendula beeches. With bony pointed
Hunching shoulders, high-hopping knees
And contorted hips, they support
Drooping drapes of layered cloaks
Of leaves worn like widows weeds
Trailing ground, completely concealing
Bark. Contents of thunderclap
Cloudbursts weigh heavily on leaves
And wash roofs orange, cream and green
Below.

Towering, tall helmeted,
Up in *Kralovska* Garden
Two green dignitary beeches
Greet north gate entrants.
Down by Belevedere summer palace,
Thickset commoner is accompanied
By slimmer oriental.
Sky light is filtered
From shuffling high shoots
Of bright light green
Mingling with copper as dark and light
As Bohemian beers - roots entangled,
Upper branches fondling.

Jackdaws lope in *Petrin* Parks'
Orchard fields. Red squirrel runs
Through lilac scent at foot of *Petrin*
Woods. Way up among woodpeckers

On virtually vertical
Hillside under *Strahovska*
Dozens of beeches have taken root.
They rise acutely angled to land -
Smooth dark sandy
Stone surface crags
Patched with cushion moss.

Above these, at very top,
Where little but sycamore
Thrive - one of very few:
Dark lattice-crack barked,
Neither broad nor tall,
With dry darkish green leaves
On brown twigs - it hovers
Over footpath, yards from planky
Logs heaped and hotchpotch:
Awaiting woodworks?

Mile or so along and across river,
Vysehrad really is headland ledge.
Woozy on promontories like this
Are unwilling to examine
Cliff drop woods. However,
Here is very thing. On *Sobeslavova*,
Mere stick's throw into *Vltava*:
Novel grove - fifteen sapling beeches,
Shape of pampas brushes,
Held in frames of wooden posts.

Search in Spain
May 2002

The plan was to see some in Spain.
It flew in the face of a sane
Concern for hard facts of the case.
In order to find the right place,
Elaborate planning increased -
Four methods of transport at least -
To fix where the focus should be:
The capital, peaks, or the sea:
All three - in time, each in whose turn
Would demonstrate talents to spurn
The beech spotter. Botanists hid
Arboreta in Madrid.
The railway's Cantabrian height
Shades forests that seem to take flight.
The beeches should scrape at the train,
But beech woods are secret in Spain.
Bright broad leaves on rock slopes are passed -
The Talgo too tinted, too fast.
(Slovenia was much the same -
With similar objects of blame.)
Street-planted on ground near the coast,
The coppers are thin as a post.
Santander: a Citroën is hired.
By this time the planner is tired.
The road sign directions conform
To some sort of non-British norm.
The map is a small masterpiece -

Yet trust in its graphics must cease.
The symbols, purporting to show
Respectively where which trees grow,
Lead up into areas where
The beeches are not merely rare:
The beeches are simply not there.
No doubt they are not far away,
But not to be found on the day.
Plans drop into pure disarray
At a nature park. *Hola!* Hello.
Surprised at the word *hayas* - lo -
The man on the gate asserts *No.*

Bedfordshire

June 2001

East enough to flatten,
West enough to wood,
Bedford probes its pattern.
Sundon's tops behood.

To neutralise the nervy,
To - peradventure - please,
Landmarks like in Turvey
Herald Luton's trees.

Derbyshire

June 2001

The region, for a ravishing display,
Seems capable of any kind of hill.
The major part's geology is grey.
Deciduous, the woods erupt and spill
Into the dales and deep-cut valley turns,
Forming on soft green western points a frill,
Or penned in low stone walls. The passer yearns
To pause, but is committed to a goal -
A hasty destination out of greed.
Snatching sylvan vistas round the whole,
The passer meets the impasse of a need.
Then in the end, the outset is clairvoyant.
The race - if only paced along a path -
Produces at the finish - gay, flamboyant,
Mozartian - a star at Matlock Bath.
The riverside is audience to this.
The crescent bend to galleries gives rise -
Green auditorium. You cannot miss,
A fifth part up the heights that lift the eyes,
An artist in the operatic school.
Waving its bushy branches like a prize,
It dances in the breeze, a great green jewel.

Sherwood Forest

June 2001

Marketing maligns
The packaging of pines -
The blocks of broad-leaf woods
Off-loaded service goods.
Undergrowths are traps
Of which existing maps
Can only form in minds
Of conservators' kinds.
Near Blidworth, on a slope,
Farm trees fulfil the scope
Of space: beech trunk's immense
And concave lines, and hence
The convex wings are spread
Umbrella-like - well-bred.

Lancaster

June 2001

Its catchment, of Pennines, fells, the sea,
Makes it a capital place to be.
Bright green slopes fall in a sweeping
Motion. Remoter, darkly leaping
Peaks hold back. Plateaux and brows
Carry woods. Meadows hold cows.

Martins dart along the Lune
As rabbits jump - jerkings of June.
Every angle traces trees -
Rippling in the cool north breeze,
Massed on banks. Or, much more sparse -
Clustered or single all grounded in grass.

Dorset

August 2001

To the north out of Studland, the fork
For the Swanage road pinches the walk
By a rare beech, grey, rounded as pork.
Its mid-trunk is much punctured. The mark
Is a circular lesion, small, dark,
At irregular points on the bark.
- On to Corfe - and a grey dry stone wall -
And behind, thick-leaved, not very tall,
A confusion of thin limbs is all
Of such beech as can promptly be found
In the town. - On to Wareham. Full-crowned
And immensely broad-based on the ground,
Far twinned coppers front recessed red houses.
- Towards Hampshire, the beech-seeker browses:
Bright magenta, the heather arouses
Intimations of ancient collection.
Sudden outcrops provoke interjection,
And, in travelling terms, resurrection.

Burnham

August 2002

One square mile -
Versatile.

Kept, perforce -
Rugged, coarse.

Heath, wood, pond
Pack a bond.

Leaf weights plumb -
Ruddy, some.

Mohaired fruits.
Moss-masked roots.

Lone to last
Fatten vast.

Young, less thick,
Outward stick.

Beech being
Forms freeing.

Volition's
Omissions.

Basel to Bern

August 2003

Cream and orange coloured,
Cracked sandstones gape
From hillside faces.

Wavy and smooth as robes
Of silk, slopes are laid
In parched grass pasture.

Growing higher, hills
Darken in the sun's
High white light.

Broadleaved woodlands
Climb rampant across
The rounded ridges.

Beeches fringe conifers,
Infiltrating a darker
Prevalence and prominence.

Foliage pulsates
In motions of breeze.
Mixed woods encroach.

Over sharpened ridges,
Like puffed quilts,
Loads of beeches flow.

Windsor Forest

September 2002

The park imparts a custody to air
The flight paths of the aeroplanes impair.
Venerated oaks eclipse
Far field vistas - hillocks, dips.
Their medieval verity is rare.

But beeches are catastrophist, some say,
And, little pollarded, soon fall away.
Tendencies, too highly strung,
Cause their kind to wither young.
Here's hardly make two hundred years today.

Fenced forestry can seem a sort of store.
Here is a hedge - suggesting something more
Cordial. A cord square-clipped,
Custody is hence equipped
Indigenous. Above, the long boughs pour.

The shoots drop, somnolent or sad. We who
Rush on the road are enervated too -
Glimpsing thick green grass and ferns
Through new gold. The season turns.
Tempting catastrophes we travel through.

Wiltshire

October 1989

A famously brooding landscape
Unleavened by a sulky sky -
A dismal outlook sinks the visitor
To defeat.

A shelterbelt of beeches
Bides
Into a feeling of friendship.

I can remember some kindlier sky,
Somewhere around the Salisbury Plain,
On one of those journeys taken to Wales,
In one of those cars that under-chugged
Our childhood.

We stopped by a sun-sweetened stand
And I wandered among some trees
Which seemed to exhale the very breath
Of unharmable contentment.

Warwickshire

October 2002

Old woody Arden
Clutches to knolls
Over a garden
Dipscape for dolls.

Blurred in a bunching
Brown gold is beech,
Meshed in a hunching
Sight strains to breach.

Hampshire Downs

November 2002

Sky seems cantilevered
Stretching to the east,
Blue with soft side wedging
Brackets, long white fleeced.
Light, in mild transition
After noon before
Dusk foreshadows fair air's
Timing to withdraw.

High on Hawkley Hanger
In a gold brown heap
Beech leaves bed in bankdrops
Falling down to Steep.
Facing, hay-pale wheat-white
Brush-bush grassy scrub
Spreads the steep near distance -
Birch, thorn, hazel shrub.
Lean among the light beige
Flashes - yellow, gold -
Represent positions
Beech has taken hold.

On the west-most downland
Beeches thin and bare
Stand all close together.
No collapsing there.
Or down on the northern
Slope. Long orange brown,
Oval in the bowl sweep:
A collective crown.

Charnwood Forest

December 2002

Gaunt oaks huddle
In troughs; on crags -
Angular muddle
Of twig-net rags.
Bark's furrows fade
To beechish flat.
Beeches invade -
But few are fat.

Girl Beech

May 1993

Beach. I often heard the name.
Too many times I'd ask
For clues to your identity -
Perfume to a cask.

I tasted salt and candy floss.
My heart beat to the sound
Of crunching shingle, dance on sand.
I felt the breeze abound.

You might have been any of many of them -
The long-haired leggy crowd
Who swept into the library -
Described once as a cloud.

Pointing, I would ask your friend,
As he spoke or smiled to each
Of a multitude of borrowers,
"Is she the one called Beach?"

Eventually I learned. You
Were the one with the wide-brimmed hat,
The owlish tortoise-shell glasses. I longed
To be somewhere you were at.

Somehow the look, intellectual,
Dramatic and *distrait,*
Did not quite match the impression
That the term was supposed to convey.

Then I discovered the spelling:
The bookish double e.
The word and the woman fell into place.
The shingle slipped into the sea.

One day you staggered through the doors
Weighed down by eighteen books,
Monumentally overdue.
We exchanged beseeching looks.

I altered the date stamp. I hid the books.
I shelved them all myself.
You said, "You've saved my life." I felt
As if I'd become Keith Relf.

I asked for your surname in order to rig
The record on your reader's card.
You confessed pretensions that elevated
You in my regard.

The name was the surname. Few people knew you
As anything more than Beech.
I promised I'd never divulge the preceding
Figures of private speech.

I never got to know you well.
We always said hello.
You fell out with our mutual friend,
And three ways we would go.

We each departed, and ever since
I have not heard the name -
While all the time I've wished that I
Could have been called the same.